Mad about

Deadly
Creatures

written by Anita Ganeri
illustrated by Sue Hendra and Paul Linnet

consultants: The Zoological Society of London (ZSL)
zsl.org

A catalogue record for this book is available from the British Library

Published by Ladybird Books Ltd
80 Strand London WC2R 0RL
A Penguin Company

2 4 6 8 10 9 7 5 3 1
© LADYBIRD BOOKS LTD MMIX

LADYBIRD and the device of a Ladybird are trademarks of Ladybird Books Ltd

ISBN: 978-1-40930-107-3

Printed in China

Contents

Some words appear in **bold** in this book.
Turn to the glossary to learn about them.

Why are creatures deadly?

The animal world can be a very dangerous place to live. Many animals have sharp teeth, **stings** or **fangs** to catch **prey** or keep **predators** away. However, most animals do not attack people unless they are hungry, surprised or frightened.

A tiger's razor-sharp teeth and claws are very dangerous. Tigers knock their prey to the ground with their paws, then kill it by biting into its neck.

Many animals use deadly **poison** to defend themselves or kill prey for food.

fangs

If you have a computer, you can download a poster of different deadly creatures from www.ladybird.com/madabout

fangs

Venomous snakes and spiders have **venom** in their fangs.

Stingrays are found in warm seas around the world. They get their name from the long, thin spike on their tails that they use to stab an attacker.

7

Dangerous bears

Bears may look cuddly, but they also have huge, powerful bodies with long, curved claws and sharp teeth. Bears use these features to kill and find food, and to defend their cubs.

Black bears live in forests throughout North America. They are excellent climbers, using their short, sharp claws to grip tree trunks. They climb trees to find food, such as honey. Baby bears also climb to get out of danger while the mother fights or runs to safety.

Grizzly bears are found in North America, Russia and Eastern Europe. They use their sharp, pointed claws like fishhooks to grab salmon from rivers. They also dig up roots and small **rodents** from underground burrows. Grizzlies will only attack people if they think their cubs are in danger.

The most dangerous bears are polar bears. They live in and around the Arctic Ocean and are the biggest meat-eaters on land. They usually eat seals, but they may also **stalk** and hunt people if they are very hungry and there is no other food around.

9

Big cats

Big cats have bodies that are perfectly suited for hunting and catching prey. Their speed and strength, and their sharp claws and teeth help them to catch animals such as deer, zebra and antelope.

Female lions in Africa and India hunt together. First, they quietly creep up on their prey. Then one lioness suddenly **pounces** and pulls the prey to the ground.

Usually, big cats do not think of humans as prey. Man-eaters tend to be old or ill animals that have found humans much easier to catch. It is very rare for this to happen.

In North America, cougars (also known as mountain lions) hunt deer, **elk** and bighorn sheep. Cougars are usually very shy, but they have sometimes been known to kill people, probably mistaking them for deer.

A leopard lies across a tree branch, waiting for an antelope to walk by. Then the leopard drops down and grabs the antelope with its powerful paws.

11

Alligators and crocodiles

Alligators and crocodiles are **reptiles** that live in swamps, rivers and lakes. They hunt many different animals, from fish to monkeys and buffalo. Their deadliest features are their speed, strength and terrifying teeth.

A saltwater crocodile measures up to 10 metres long and weighs more than 1.5 tonnes. This deadly hunter can catch prey as big as a horse. It is also thought to kill about two thousand people a year. Saltwater crocodiles live in South-East Asia and Australia.

How a crocodile hunts

1. A crocodile floats in the water, looking like a harmless log.

2. When an antelope comes close to the shore, the crocodile leaps out of the water and grabs the antelope in its massive jaws.

3. The crocodile drags it under water to drown, rolling over and over until its victim is dead. This is called a 'death-roll'.

You can tell the difference between an alligator and a crocodile by looking at their teeth.

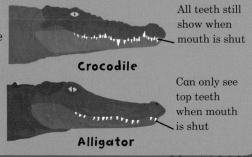

All teeth still show when mouth is shut

Crocodile

Can only see top teeth when mouth is shut

Alligator

Deadly sea creatures

The great white shark is a fearsome hunter that has been known to attack people. It can bite its prey clean in half with its rows of sharp, jagged teeth.

The box jellyfish is only as big as a football but its venom is very strong. Its stinging **tentacles** are extremely painful and can kill a person in fewer than three minutes.

Stonefish live on the seabed and are difficult to see as they look just like rocks. If they are disturbed, they squirt out a deadly venom through the spines on their fins.

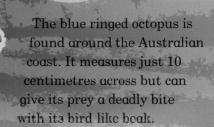

The blue ringed octopus is found around the Australian coast. It measures just 10 centimetres across but can give its prey a deadly bite with its bird like beak.

Cone shells in the Indian and Pacific Oceans eat fish or worms that they spear with their dart-like teeth. The teeth are loaded with venom strong enough to kill a person.

A puffer fish can puff up its body to about three times its normal size, making its spines stick up. These spines are painful, but the puffer fish is only deadly if it is eaten. In fact, one puffer fish contains enough poison to kill thirty adults.

Spiders and scorpions

Some spiders, such as tarantulas, hunt for insects to eat. Other spiders catch their prey in webs. The spiders kill their prey with venom from their needle-sharp fangs. Scorpions are related to spiders and are known for their stinging tails.

Black widow spiders found in North America, South Africa and Australia are small but deadly. They grab their insect prey in their fangs and hold on to it for several minutes until the venom works.

A deadly funnel-web spider from Australia spins a
funnel-shaped web over its underground burrow.
If an insect walks across,
it shakes the web and
the spider rushes out of
its burrow for the kill.

Scorpions keep their venom in
the tip of their tails, which they
curl over their heads to strike.
They use their stings to kill
prey and to protect themselves.

17

Scary snakes

Snakes eat other animals, such as mice, birds, frogs and even deer. They have two ways of killing their prey. Some snakes use venom and others squeeze their prey to death.

Cobras live in Africa and Asia, and are very venomous. The king cobra's venom is so strong that it can kill an elephant in three hours.

King cobra

The deadliest snake is the inland taipan, from Australia. A single bite has enough venom to kill one hundred adults, but it is shy and rarely seen.

A snake's fangs are long, sharp, hollow teeth. Some snakes have fangs that fold away when they are not being used, and swing forward when the snake is about to strike.

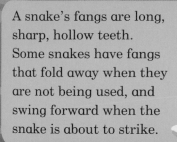

Some snakes, such as boas and pythons, wrap their strong bodies around their prey and squeeze it to death. They can also stretch their jaws extremely wide, which means that they can swallow their prey whole.

19

Sharp stingers

Wasps and bees use venomous stings as weapons. Their stings are sharp, hollow spikes on their abdomens. When a bee or wasp stings, it pumps venom through the spike into its victim.

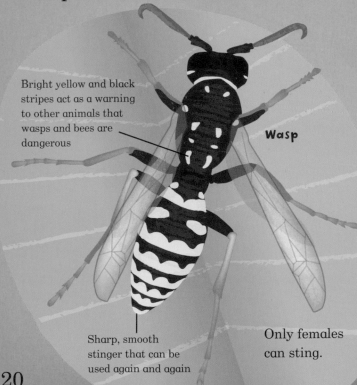

Bright yellow and black stripes act as a warning to other animals that wasps and bees are dangerous

Wasp

Sharp, smooth stinger that can be used again and again

Only females can sting.

Bees can only sting once. Their stings are covered in tiny hooks that stick fast to skin. When a honeybee tries to withdraw its sting, it is instead torn from its body. Without this it will die.

bee sting

Most bees will only sting if something disturbs them. The most dangerous bee is a kind of honeybee that attacks in **swarms**. A swarm of bees can kill a person.

Prickles and spines

Some animals have bodies that are covered in deadly-looking prickles, spines and **quills**. These are dangerous weapons for scaring away enemies.

A sea urchin is a creature found in oceans all over the world.

A sea urchin's spines are venomous. They stick into an attacker's skin, leaving a painful wound. Apart from self-defence, sea urchins also use their spines for moving about and burrowing into the seabed.

Porcupines are found in North and South America, Asia and Europe. A porcupine's back and tail are covered in thousands of needle-sharp quills. If a porcupine is threatened, it rattles its quills to frighten an attacker away. If this doesn't work, it lashes out with its prickly tail.

The thorny devil is a lizard that lives in the Australian desert. It looks fierce because its skin is covered from head to food in sharp spikes. The spikes protect the lizard from attack.

23

Deadly people

The deadliest creatures in the world are not sharks, bears or snakes. They are human beings! All over the world, people are destroying natural **habitats** and killing animals.

Each year, people cut down and burn huge numbers of rainforest trees. Many amazing animals live in the rainforest and can become **extinct** when their homes are destroyed.

24

People are dumping so much rubbish in the seas that it is putting animals at risk. In the Pacific Ocean, many albatrosses are dying because they eat plastic by mistake.

For years, people have hunted animals such as tigers, crocodiles and snakes for their skins and other body parts. So many tigers have been killed that they are almost extinct.

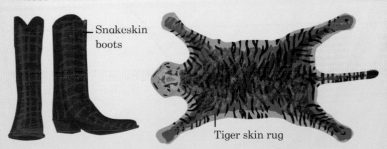

Snakeskin boots

Tiger skin rug

People need to look after animals and take care of their habitats. You can help by joining a **conservation** group that helps to pick up litter from beaches, for example.

Fantastic factfile

- Some kinds of cobras spit venom into their enemies' eyes. They can aim with amazing accuracy from up to 3 metres away.

- In 1898, two man-eating lions in Africa killed and ate 135 people who were building a new railway.

- The Portuguese man-of-war is related to jellyfish. Its tentacles can be more than 50 metres long and are loaded with venomous stings.

- The plague is a terrible disease that killed millions of people in the past. It was spread by the tiny fleas that live on black rats.

- A bulldog ant from Australia is doubly dangerous. It holds onto its victim with its jagged jaws. Then it curls its body under and gives a painful sting!

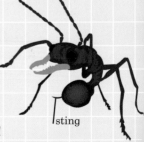

sting

A hippopotamus's huge lower teeth are deadly weapons. When they fight, male hippos open their mouths wide and lunge at each other with their teeth.

Only two kinds of lizards are poisonous. These are the gila monster from North America and Mexico, and the Mexican bearded lizard. They bite into prey, then keep chewing to work the poison in.

gila monster

Sharks only kill about ten people a year, but people kill around 100 million (100,000,000) sharks! Some sharks are hunted for their fins which are then turned into shark-fin soup.

Some crocodiles can catch animals as large as a buffalo.

A single drop of poison from the skin of the poison arrow frog is enough to kill a large monkey.

Amazing awards

Fiercest fish

The razor-toothed piranha is the fiercest freshwater fish in the world. A group of these piranhas could strip a cow to the bone in a few minutes.

Deadliest spider

The Brazilian wandering spider is the deadliest spider alive. One teaspoon of its venom could kill 83,000 mice!

Shortest venomous snake

A spotted dwarf adder only grows up to 24 centimetres long, about twenty times smaller than the king cobra, the biggest venomous snake. Despite its size, it can still kill small **mammals** and birds.

spotted dwarf adder —

⭐ Longest fangs

A gaboon viper s fangs can measure up to 5 centimetres. That's as long as your little finger.

⭐ Only poisonous bird

The pitohui is the only poisonous bird we know of. Its feathers and skin are poisonous enough to kill mice and frogs.

⭐ Deadliest insect

A mosquito is tiny but it is the most dangerous insect on Earth. It spreads a disease called malaria that kills millions of people every year.

Glossary

conservation – the protection of nature, animals and plants.

elk – a type of large deer that lives in North America and Asia.

extinct – when a type of animal or plant dies out.

fangs – long, hollow teeth through which some animals, such as snakes, inject venom.

habitat – the natural home of plants or animals.

mammal – an animal with a backbone and hair or fur, that gives birth to live young.

poison – a dangerous substance that is eaten or absorbed through the skin.

pounce – to jump out suddenly at an animal during hunting.

predator – animals that hunt, kill and eat other animals.

prey – animals that are killed and eaten by other animals.

quills – the long, sharp spines covering a porcupine's body.

reptile – animals with dry, scaly skin, such as snakes and crocodiles.

rodents – animals, such as mice, rats and squirrels, that have large front teeth.

stalk – to hunt prey by quietly creeping after it.

sting – a sharp, hollow part of a creature, such as a wasp, bee, scorpion or ant, that is used to pierce flesh and inject venom.

swarm – large groups of insects, such as wasps or bees.

tentacles – long, dangling parts of an animal, such as a jellyfish, that are used to feel, grab and inject venom.

venom – a dangerous substance that is injected, usually through a bite or sting.